YOUNG CHEF

COOK BOOK

VEER SOLANKI

Contents

Contents

1

Yogurt crunchy puddings

ingredients:-

- 400 gms hung yogurt
- 2 tbsp fresh rose water
- 1 tbsp organic honey
- 1/2 cup grapes, chopped
- 1/2 cup strawberries, chopped
- 1/2 cup pomegranate kernels
- 2 tbsp butter
- A pinch of ground cinnamon
- 2 tsp finely ground cane sugar
- Brandy (optional)
- Base:
- 1 cup dried breadcrumbs/crushed ragi biscuits

Procedure:-

- Put together the cane sugar, breadcrumbs, and a pinch of cinnamon with butter in a bowl and rub between your fingers.
- Lay out the dry mixture in a flat dish as the base of the pudding.
- Mix the hung yogurt, honey, rose water, chopped strawberries, and chopped grapes and lather it on the base, topping it with crushed pistachios and pomegranates, and allow to set in the

fridge.

2

Plum milkshake

ingredients:-

- 200 Gram Plum
- 100 Gram Dates
- 80 Gram Sugar
- 200 Ml Water
- 800 Ml Milk

procedure:-

1. Put all the above ingredients in a stainless-steel pot on medium heat and boil for 15 minutes until soft.
2. Let the syrup cool then blend until the concentrated syrup is ready.
3. It stays in the fridge for later use.
4. Boil milk and make it cool.
5. In a mixing bowl take milk.
6. Add above Sharbat and 10/15 ice cubes in milk
7. Mix well and serve cool.

3

Soya pulao

ingredients:-

- 1 Cup Soya Chunks
- 250 gram Soaked Rice
- 1/2 cup Curd
- 1 tbsp Ginger Garlic Paste
- 1 medium Chopped Onion
- 1 medium Chopped Tomato
- 2 Slit Green Chillies
- 1 Cardamom
- 2-3 Green Cardamom
- 8-10 Black Pepper
- 7-8 Cloves
- 1 Bay Leaf
- 2 Whole Red Chilli
- 2 tsp Red Chilli Powder
- 2 tsp Coriander Powder
- 1 tsp Cumin Powder
- 1/2 tsp Turmeric
- 1 tsp Chicken Masala
- 1/2 tsp Garam Masala
- 3 tbsp Vegetable Oil
- to taste Salt

Procedure :-

1. First of all, soak soya chunks in hot water for 15 minutes. After 15 minutes, squeeze the soya chunks out of the water and separate them.
2. Now take soya chunks in the vessel, add curd, red chili, ginger-garlic paste, coriander powder and mix it well and keep it aside for some time.
3. Heat oil in a pressure cooker, add all the whole spices, and whole red chili, and fry for a few seconds. After this add chopped onion and fry for a few seconds.
4. Add marinated soya chunks with onions and fry for some time. After this add chopped tomatoes and green chilies and cook it till it becomes soft.
5. Add red chili powder, coriander powder, garam masala, turmeric, and salt as per taste, and cook everything well.
6. Add the soaked rice to the spices, mix it well and cover the pressure cooker with water as needed.
7. After two whistles, turn off the gas and after the pressure is released, take out the prepared casserole in a serving bowl and serve it. Pair it with raita or chutney.

4

Mac and cheese

ingredients:-

- 1/3 cup macaroni
- 3/4 cup cheddar cheese, shredded
- 2 tbsp milk
- 1/4 cup water

Procedure:-

1. Take macaroni in a bowl and add water to it.
2. Microwave the bowl for about two minutes.
3. Add milk and shredded cheese to the macaroni, and stir a little.
4. Microwave the bowl for another minute.
5. Your delicious Mac & Cheese is ready to eat hot.

5

Chilli cheese toast

Ingredients:-

- 1 cup cheese - grated
- 1 tsp salt
- chili powder - to taste
- 1 tbsp coriander leaves
- green chilies - chopped (to taste)
- 1 tsp baking powder
- milk - as required
- 6 bread slices
- oil - for deep frying

Procedure:-

1. Mix the cheese, salt, chilli powder, coriander, green chilies, baking powder, and enough milk to beat to a thick batter, till well blended and light.
2. Keep aside in a cool place for at least half an hour.
3. Cut off the edges of the slices and divide each into halves.
4. Pile the cheese mixture over the slices.
5. Heat oil till a little bit of the batter thrown in comes up at once.
6. Drop the bread pieces into it. Brown on both sides and serve hot.

6

new york cheesecake

Ingredients:-

- 15 Graham crackers, crushed
- 2 tbsp Butter, melted
- 4 (8 ounces) packages of cream cheese
- 1 and a half cups White sugar
- 3/4 cups Milk
- 4 Eggs
- 1 cup Sour cream
- 1/4 cup all-purpose flour
- 1 tbsp Vanilla extract

Procedure:-

1. Preheat the oven to 350 degrees F (175 degrees C). Grease a 9-inch springform pan.
2. Mix graham cracker crumbs and melted butter together in a medium bowl until well combined; press onto the bottom of the prepared pan to make a packed crust.
3. Mix cream cheese and sugar together in a large bowl until smooth. Blend in milk, then mix in eggs, one at a time, until just combined. Add sour cream, flour, and vanilla; mix until smooth. Pour filling onto prepared crust.

4. Bake in preheated oven for 1 hour. Turn the oven off; let cheesecake cool in the oven with the door closed for 5 to 6 hours to prevent cracking.
5. Chill in the refrigerator until serving.

7

Chole Bhature

Ingredients

- 2 cup chickpeas (channas)
- 2 tsp oil
- 1 bay leaf (tej patta)
- 1 Cinnamon stick (dalchini)
- 3-4 Cloves (laung)
- 1 tsp whole peppercorns (sabut kali mirch)
- 3 Green cardamom (choti elaichi)
- 2 Black cardamom (badi elaichi)
- 1 tsp turmeric powder (haldi)
- 1 tsp chili powder (lal mirch powder)
- 1 tsp coriander powder (dhaniya powder)
- 1 tsp cumin powder (jeera powder)
- 1 tsp cumin seeds (jeera)
- 1/2 tsp asafoetida (heeng)
- to taste salt
- 1 cup onions, chopped
- 1 cup tomatoes, chopped
- 1 tsp ginger, chopped
- 1 tsp garlic, chopped
- 1 tsp ajwain
- 1 tsp lime juice

- 1 green chili, chopped
- 1 Teabag
- 1 tbsp butter
- For the bhaturas:
- 2 cups maida (refined flour)
- 1/2 tsp yeast (dissolved for 10 minutes in lukewarm water)
- 1/2 cup whole wheat flour
- A pinch of salt
- Water (to knead)
- Oil (for frying)

Procedure:-

1. In a pan add oil, bay leaf, cinnamon, cumin seeds, cloves, whole pepper corns, green and black cardamom.
2. After it gets brown add chopped onions and saute it. Now add chopped ginger and garlic.
3. Followed by turmeric, chili powder, coriander powder, cumin powder, asafoetida and salt, fry the ingredients together well.
4. For deglazing the pan add a little water.
5. Now add the chole (soaked overnight and pressure cooked) to the masala.
6. After stirring well add tomatoes, little sugar and salt to the chole.
7. Now add ajwain, chopped green chilies and water for the base.
8. To get the color in the chole, add a tea bag to the masala.
9. Simmer the chole gently for an hour and cover it.
10. Add lime juice and a dollop of butter to it.
11. Garnish the chole with coriander and butter and serve them hot with bhaturas.
12. Prepare the bhaturas:
13. Knead the whole wheat flour, maida and salt together with adequate amount of water.
14. Sprinkle the yeast on top. Leave it for 2-3 hours for the yeast to work.
15. Divide it into equal portions. Roll out in an oval or round shape.

16. Deep fry till golden brown, like a puri.
17. Serve.

8

Paneer Tika

Ingredients:-

- 1/2 Kg paneer
- 1 tomato
- 1 onion
- 1 capsicum
- Marinade for paneer tikka:
- 1/2 tbsp cumin seeds
- 1/2 tbsp coriander seeds
- 1 brown cardamom
- 10 green cardamom
- 1/2 tbsp cloves
- 1/2 tbsp black pepper
- 2 pcs star anise
- 1/2 tbsp shahee zeera
- 3 tbsp ginger-garlic paste
- 2 tsp turmeric powder
- 2 tsp red chilli powder
- 2 tsp coriander powder
- Salt
- 2 tsp kashmiri chilli powder
- 2 tbsp refined oil
- 1/2 lime

- 1/2 tbsp dry mango powder
- 1/2 tbsp chaat masala
- 2 green chilli, chopped
- 100 gms curd (whisked)
- 1/2 tbsp garam masala
- coriander leaves, chopped
- mint leaves, chopped

Procedure:-

- Dry roast and pound cumin seeds, coriander seeds, brown cardamom, green cardamom, cloves, black pepper, star anise and shahee zeera in a mortar and pestle.
- In a bowl add ginger garlic paste, turmeric powder, red chilli powder, coriander powder, salt, Kashmiri chilli powder, refined oil, coriander leaves chopped, mint leaves chopped, lime, dry mango powder, chaat masala, green chilli, whisked curd and hara masala. Mix them all.
- For grilling paneer tikka:
- In a tray spread some paneer cubes, julienne onion, capsicum and tomatoes.
- Mix the masala in the tray. Marinate the paneer cubes.
- Skewer the tikkas for roasting.
- Now keep the marinated paneer tikkas in the fridge for 45 minutes.
- Then grill the tikkas till cooked.
- Serve the paneer tikka hot.

9

Chocolate cake

Ingredients:-

- 3 Tbsp all-purpose flour/maida
- 3 Tbsp powdered sugar
- 1 Tbsp unsweetened cocoa
- 2 Tbsp crushed oreo cookies
- 1/8 tsp baking powder
- 1/2 tsp salt
- 1/4 tsp vanilla extract
- 3 Tbsp oil / melted butter
- 3 Tbsp milk (you might require less)

Procedure:-

1. Mix flour, sugar, cocoa, baking powder, and salt in the mug.
2. Add vanilla, crushed cookies, milk, and oil and make the batter.
3. Make sure that your mug is only half full so that the cake has some space to rise and be fluffy.
4. Microwave it for 1 minute on the highest power.
5. Note: The timing may vary according to your microwave setting and your mug too. So insert a knife or toothpick after 1 minute and if it comes out clean your one-minute cake is ready, if not then microwave for 30 more seconds. And that's about it, you

are done. Now, I know we feel like eating our cakes at that very moment, but wait for a few minutes, just a few and dig into it while it is warm.

10

coconut balls

Ingredients:-

- 4 cups grated coconut, desiccated
- 1/2 cup milk powder
- 1 tin condensed milk
- 1 tbsp ghee
- 1/2 tsp cardamom powder
- A few tbsps of desiccated coconut to garnish

Procedure:-

1. Heat 1/2 tbsp ghee in a heavy-bottomed vessel.
2. Add coconut and saute for 4-5 minutes on low flame.
3. Add 1/2 cup milk powder and a tin of condensed milk and keep stirring constantly (on low flame) till it starts leaving the sides of the vessel, approx 8-10 minutes.
4. Add 1/2 tsp cardamom powder and mix. Turn off the heat and cool.
5. Grease your hand, make small coconut ladoo balls, and roll in desiccated coconut.

Tips: In an air-tight container, place the balls in your fridge for longer shelf life. At room temperature, they stay fresh for up to 2-3 days.

11

Chilli Gobi

Ingredients :-

- 500 Gram Cauliflower (gobhi, cut into small florets)
- 2 tsp Salt
- 1 Egg
- 1/2 cup Corn flour
- 1 tsp Ginger-garlic paste
- To mix the batter Water
- For deep frying Oil
- 2 cups Onions , finely chopped
- 2 tbsp Green chillies , sliced
- 1 tbsp Soya sauce
- 2 tbsp Vinegar
- Some greens for garnish

Procedure :-

1. Mix together the gobhi, 1 teaspoon salt, egg, corn flour, garlic, ginger and enough water to have the pieces coated with the mixture.
2. Heat the oil, and fry over medium heat to a golden color.
3. Heat 2 tbsp of the oil in a wok, and stir fry the onions in it over high heat till they look wet.

4. Add the green chillies and stir a few times, add the remaining salt, soya sauce, vinegar, and the gobhi.
5. Mix well, and serve garnished with some greens.

Tip- If you like the gobhi softer, you can blanch it before adding it to the batter ingredients.

12

Kashmiri Paneer

Ingredients:-

- 1/2 Tbsp oil
- 3 cloves
- 1 bay leaf
- 1 cinnamon stick
- 1 tsp cumin seeds
- 3 green cardamom
- 1 Tbsp sund powder (Dry ginger powder)
- 1 Tbsp saunf powder
- 1 glass milk
- Salt, to taste
- Pepper, to taste
- 1/4 th glass water
- 300 gm paneer, cut into large chunks and deep fried
- Coriander leaves, chopped, to garnish

Procedure:-

1. In a wok add oil, bay leaf, cloves, green cardamom, cinnamon stick and cumin seeds. Let it splutter.
2. Add the saunf and sund powder. Saute vigorously. Do not let it burn.

3. Immediately add the milk and water. Let it come to a boil and add salt and pepper.
4. Add the deep fried paneer chunks. Let it simmer for 5 minutes.
5. Garnish with coriander leaves.
6. Serve with dum aloo, mooli ki chutney and steamed rice.

Note: Let this dish rest for about 20-30 minutes before serving so that the paneer can soak up the milk and becomes soft & flavorful.

13

Garlic egg Fried rice

Ingredients:-

- 2 Tbsp oil
- 1 Egg
- 1 tsp ginger, chopped
- 6-7 Garlic cloves (mashed)
- 1 red chilli, chopped
- 2 cups rice, steamed
- 1 tsp salt
- 1 tsp black pepper powder
- 1 tsp soya sauce
- 1 tsp coriander, chopped
- 2 tsp spring onion, chopped

Procedure:-

1. Heat oil in a pan on medium flame and add the chopped garlic to it. Cook until lightly golden.
2. Now add a teaspoon of spring onion, ginger, and red chili. Saute for a minute.
3. Break an egg in the pan. Mix and cook until scrambled.
4. Then pour the steamed rice and combine it well with the ingredients with light hands.

5. Add salt and black pepper powder and thoroughly pour soya sauce over the rice.
6. Again add a teaspoon of spring onion to the rice and stir for a minute.
7. Transfer the hot and delicious fried rice to a bowl and serve hot garnished with spring onions and some coriander leaves.

14

Matar Kebab

Ingredients:-

- 500 gms spinach (squeezed), blanched
- 500 gms peas, boiled
- 2 green chilies, chopped
- 1 tbsp ginger, chopped
- to taste salt
- 1/4 tsp black pepper, powdered
- 2 bread slices, grated
- Chickpea flour (gram flour), to dust kebabs
- Oil, to pan fry

Procedure:-

1. Place the peas, spinach, ginger, green chilies and bread in the blender and puree.
2. Mix in the salt and black pepper.
3. Shape the mixture into rounds and dust with the chickpea flour.
4. Heat a thin layer of oil in a frying pan and brown the kababs on both sides.
5. Serve garnished with onion rings.

15

Quick Quesadilla

Ingredients:-

- 2 chappatis / roti (leftover)
- 3 tbsp onion, finely chopped
- 3 tbsp tomato, finely chopped
- 3 tbsp capsicum, finely chopped
- 3-4 olives, sliced
- 1 cheese single
- butter for frying
- to taste salt
- to taste red chili
- to taste oregano
- to taste red chili sauce

Procedure:-

1. Mix onions, tomatoes, capsicum, and olives.
2. Add salt, red chili, and red chili sauce as per taste.
3. Heat a pan and some butter.
4. Place one roti on the pan.
5. Add the filling and the cheese single.
6. Place the roti over the filling and press slightly.
7. Add more butter and flip the roti to cook from another side.

8. Cook until the chapatis are a little crisp and the cheese melts.

16

Vada Pao

Ingredients:-

- For potato mix:
- 1 cup potatoes (boiled and mashed)
- 1 tbsp garlic, finely chopped
- 1 tsp ginger, finely chopped
- 1 tsp cumin seeds
- 1 tbsp coriander cumin powder
- 1 tsp red chilli powder / cayenne pepper
- 1/2 tsp turmeric
- 1 tbsp lime juice
- 1 tbsp oil
- to taste salt
- For fritters:
- 3/4 cup chickpea flour
- salt, to season
- 1 tsp red chillli powder
- 1 1/4 cup water
- oil to deep fry
- 3 pieces pao bread
- 1 tsp oil
- For assembling:
- 1/4 cup tamarind sauce

- 1/4 cup green chutney
- 1/8 cup sweet yogurt

Procedure:-

1. Heat oil in a pan. Once hot, add cumin seeds, chopped ginger and garlic.
2. When the garlic and ginger turn golden, add all the spice powders, salt and mashed potatoes.
3. Mix well and turn the heat off. Add the lime juice and chopped cilantro for garnish.
4. Once the potato mixture cools down, divide the mixture into 10-12 equal portions and shape them into pin pong sized balls.
5. Mix the chickpea flour, salt and chili powder. Add water in small quantities & mix well until you make a pancake (or dosa) like batter.
6. Heat up the oil for frying.
7. Coat each ball with the batter and drop into the hot oil. Do not overcrowd the oil (it brings down the temperature of oil all of a sudden).
8. When they turn golden, drain them onto some paper towels. Set Aside.
9. For the bread baskets, cut the bread into a discs using a cutter or just cut the crusts off.
10. Flatten out the bread discs slightly using a rolling pin.
11. Grease a muffin pan and set the rolled out bread discs in it.
12. Bake at 350°F for 5-7 min or until it gets toasted slightly. We do not want the bread to dry up. It has to be like toast; crispy outer layer but soft.
13. Once done, Set aside and cool the baskets for 5 minutes.
14. When you are ready to serve, start assembling the vada pav bites.
15. Place a little bit of tamarind sauce in the basket (depending on your taste), place the potato fritter on it.
16. Now, pipe some green chutney on top and sprinkle some spicy garlic chutney.

17. Elegant, mini vada pav bites are ready to be served.

17

Wendy chilli

Ingredients:-

- 1 garlic clove, minced
- 1 tablespoon olive oil
- 1 medium onion, diced
- 2 celery stalks, diced
- 1 green bell pepper, diced
- 1 lb. ground beef
- 1 tablespoon taco seasoning
- 1 10 oz can. pinto beans
- 1 10 oz. can kidney beans
- 1 10 oz. can tomato sauce
- 1 10 oz. can diced tomatoes
- Shredded cheddar cheese, for topping
- Sour cream, for topping

Procedure:-

1. Heat up a dutch oven or a stockpot over medium heat. Add in the olive oil, minced garlic, onion, celery, and green bell pepper. When the vegetables start to become soft (about three minutes), add in the ground beef.

2. Using a wooden spoon, break up the ground beef and stir in with the vegetables. When the ground beef is no longer pink, using a spoon, drain the grease into an excess can.
3. Add in the beans, tomato sauce, and diced tomatoes into the dutch oven. Sprinkle in the taco seasoning and mix together.
4. Turn the chili on simmer, and let it cook for at least 30 minutes, stirring once in a while so nothing burns at the bottom. The longer you let it sit, the better the flavors will become.
5. Serve with shredded cheese and sour cream, if desired.

18

Taco Bell Chili Cheese Burrito

Ingredients:-

- 1 lb. ground beef
- 1 tbsp taco seasoning
- 1 10 oz. can refried beans
- 1 6 oz. can tomato paste
- Shredded taco cheese
- 6 flour burrito shells

Procedure:-

1. Warm a skillet on medium heat.
2. Cook the ground beef until no longer pink. Drain the excess grease into a can.
3. Sprinkle in the taco seasoning.
4. Add the cans of refried beans and tomato paste. Stir to combine.
5. Let the chili-cheese mixture get warm before making the burrito.
6. To make the burrito, spoon on some of the chili cheese mixture and sprinkle the same amount of cheese into a burrito shell. Wrap up the burrito.

7. To press the burrito, heat up a separate skillet. Add the bottom of the burrito to it and let it sit for 1-3 minutes, or until the bottom of the burrito is toasty. Flip and toast the other side, pressing it down with a spatula.
8. Serve with your favorite hot sauce or, if you have them, leftover packets of Taco Bell sauces!

19

Smoothie King Strawberry Smoothie

Ingredients:-

- 1 1/2 cups fresh strawberries, halved
- 1 Tbsp coconut sugar
- 1/2 tsp kosher salt, divided
- 1 can coconut milk, including the water, refrigerated overnight
- 1/2 tsp vanilla extract
- 3/4 cup cashew milk, frozen overnight in ice cube tray
- 1 tsp fresh lemon juice

Procedure:-

1. Preheat oven to 350°F. Spread out strawberries on a sheet pan and toss with 2 teaspoons coconut sugar and ¼ teaspoon salt. Bake for 25 to 30 minutes, until juicy. Let cool.
2. Scoop the firm, chilled coconut cream from the top of the can into a medium bowl. Using an electric mixer, whip cream until smooth and airy. Whip in the remaining 1 teaspoon coconut sugar, ¼ teaspoon salt, and vanilla until combined. Return the bowl to the fridge.

3. Combine cooled strawberries, frozen cashew milk ice cubes, lemon juice, and ½ cup of coconut water from the can in the blender, and puree until smooth. Add more coconut water to thin the smoothie until desired consistency is reached.
4. Pour smoothie into a glass and top with a spoonful of coconut whipped cream.

20

Yogurt Parfait

Ingredients:-

- 1 cup sliced strawberries (Any juicy fruit will work well here if you want to sub in things like raspberries, blackberries, kiwi, and mangoes.)
- ½ cup blueberries (frozen are good, too)
- 2 tsp sugar
- 4–5 mint leaves, sliced thinly
- 1 container (8 oz) low-fat plain Greek-style yogurt (Fage 2% is our favorite. If you don't dig the thick Greek yogurt, any plain yogurt will work, as long as there are no added sugars.)
- ¼ cup granola

Procedure:-

1. Combine the fruit, sugar, and mint in a bowl, and allow to sit for 3 to 4 minutes.
2. Spoon half of the yogurt into a bowl or glass, then top with half of the fruit and granola, then repeat with the remaining yogurt, fruit, and granola.
3. Pour any accumulated juice from the fruit over the top.

21

Fudgy Brownie

Ingredient:-

- ½ cup (1stick) butter
- 2 oz semi-sweet dark chocolate, chopped
- ¾ cup sugar
- ½ cup unsweetened cocoa powder
- 1 ½ tsp vanilla
- 3 eggs
- ½ cup all-purpose flour
- 1 tsp baking powder
- ¾ tsp salt
- ½ cup chopped walnuts (optional)

Procedure:-

1. Preheat the oven to 350°F.
2. Melt the butter and chocolate together in a pan set over low heat.
3. Stir in the sugar, cocoa, and vanilla and remove from the heat.
4. Add the eggs, flour, baking powder, and salt and whisk until smooth. Stir in the walnuts if using.
5. Pour the batter into an 8" x 8" baking pan coated with a bit of nonstick spray.
6. Spread the batter out into an even layer.

7. Bake for 20 to 25 minutes, until a toothpick inserted in the center comes out nearly clean. (If you like your brownies less fudgy, bake a few extra minutes, until the toothpick comes out perfectly clean.)

22

Sausage Pasta

Ingredients:-

- Olive Oil
- Sausage (polish sausage, turkey kielbasa, smoked sausage etc)
- Onion
- Garlic
- Fire Roasted Tomatoes
- Uncooked Pasta
- Chicken Broth
- Milk
- Cheddar Cheese

Procedure:-

1. Everything cooks in one pan, so you don't need to worry about boiling the noodles ahead of time. Start by sautéing the onions and sausage in a large skillet until they are soft and the sausage is browned.
2. Dump everything but the cheese into the skillet and mix until it is well combined. Bring it to a boil and then cover and reduce the heat to simmer.
3. Stir a couple of times while it is cooking, and cook for about 10 minutes until the pasta is cooked and most of the liquid is

absorbed.

4. Top with the cheese and stir until it is melted. Garnish with green onions and serve immediately.

23

Browny Bites

Ingredients:-

- 4 ounces unsweetened baking chocolate coarsely chopped
- 3/4 cup unsalted butter sliced
- 1 3/4 cups sugar
- 3 large eggs
- 1 tablespoon vanilla extract
- 2 tablespoons unsweetened cocoa powder
- 1/2 teaspoon salt
- 1 cup all-purpose flour

Procedure:-

1. Preheat oven to 350°F. Spray mini muffin pans with nonstick cooking spray with flour or line with liners.
2. Place the baking chocolate and butter in a large, microwave safe bowl. Heat on HIGH power for 2-3 minutes, stirring every 30 seconds, until chocolate is smooth. Stir in sugar. Add eggs, vanilla, and cocoa and stir well. Add salt and flour and stir carefully.
3. Place about 1 heaping tablespoon of batter in each muffin cup. Bake for 10-12 minutes, until a toothpick comes out only slightly dirty from the center of the brownie.

4. If you are topping the brownie bites with candies, unwrap them while the brownies are baking. As soon as the brownie bites come out of the oven, press one candy on the top of each brownie bite, pressing slightly. Let them cool completely before removing from the pans.
5. If you are topping them with ganache, let them cool completely then remove from the pans. Make the ganache by placing the chocolate chips and cream in a microwave safe measuring cup or bowl. Heat in 30 second increments, stirring between each, until the chocolate is melted and smooth. It will be thick, like frosting. Frost each brownie bite, then top with sprinkles.

24

Maple cinnamon roles

ingredients:-

- 2/3 cup whole milk
- 1/3 cup maple syrup
- 1/3 cup butter, softened
- 1 large egg, room temperature
- 3/4 teaspoon salt
- 3 cups bread flour
- 1 package (1/4 ounce) active dry yeast

Procedure:-

1. In bread machine pan, place the first seven ingredients in order suggested by manufacturer. Select dough setting (check dough after 5 minutes of mixing; add 1 to 2 tablespoons of water or bread flour if needed).
2. When the cycle is completed, turn dough onto a lightly floured surface. Roll into two 12x7-in. rectangles. In a small bowl, combine the brown sugar, flour and cinnamon; cut in butter until mixture resembles coarse crumbs. Sprinkle half over each rectangle. Roll up jelly-roll style, starting from a long side; pinch seam to seal.

3. Cut each roll into 12 slices. Place cut side down in one greased 13x9-in. baking pan. Cover and let rise in a warm place until doubled, about 20 minutes.
4. Bake at 375° until golden brown, 20-25 minutes. Cool on a wire rack for 5 minutes. Meanwhile, in a small bowl, combine the confectioners' sugar, butter, syrup and enough milk to achieve desired consistency. Spread over warm rolls.

25

Banana Bites

ingredients:-

- 3/4 cup sugar
- 1/4 cup packed brown sugar
- 1-1/2 teaspoons ground cinnamon

Procedure:-

1. In a small bowl, mix sugars and cinnamon until blended. In a large bowl, whisk the first 5 beignet ingredients. In another bowl, whisk egg, bananas, milk and 2 tablespoons oil until blended. Add to flour mixture; stir just until moistened.
2. In an electric skillet or deep fryer, heat oil to 375°. Drop tablespoonfuls of batter, a few at a time, into hot oil. Fry about 45-60 seconds on each side or until golden brown. Drain on paper towels. Roll warm beignets in sugar mixture.

26

Pudding shots

ingredients:-

- Instant chocolate pudding– Just the dry mix!
- Milk– Cold
- Brewed coffee -Cooled
- Coffee liqueur
- Whipped topping (Cool Whip)– Thawed
- Instant white chocolate pudding- Just the dry mix!
- Vodka
- Shot glasses

Procedure:-

1. Beat together the instant chocolate pudding mix with the milk, brewed coffee, and Kahlua liqueur until combined.
2. Slowly fold in the whipped topping and then set aside.
3. In another bowl combine the white chocolate pudding mix, milk, and vodka with an electric mixer until smooth. fold in the whipped topping.
4. Place both puddings mixes into their own zip-top bags and snip a corner from both bags.
5. Carefully pipe the chocolate pudding into 12 shot glasses. fill them about halfway full.

6. Now pipe the white chocolate pudding into the glasses, filling them to the top.
7. Garnish with shaved chocolate pieces, and Pirouette Cookie halves.
8. Place the shooters in the fridge to chill for at least one hour, but up to a day.

27

Milkshake shooters

ingredients:-

- 3 scoops vanilla ice cream
- 1/2 cup marshmallow fluff
- 1/2 cup milk
- 1 teaspoon vanilla extract

Procedure:-

1. In a blender, mix together ice cream, milk, vanilla extract and marshmallow fluff.
2. For a thinner milkshake add more milk. If you'd like it a bit thicker... add more ice cream.
3. Pour the milkshakes into little glasses. You can also rim the glasses in chocolate and dip in sprinkles for an extra touch of fun!

28

Oreo Triffles

ingredients:-

- 1 cup whipping cream
- 1 teaspoon mint extract
- 4 drops of green food coloring
- 6 oreo cookies chopped
- 1 Aero mint chocolate
- 1/2 cup York minis
- 2 pudding snacks

Procedure:-

1. Add the whipping cream to your mixer and mix until stiff peaks form. Add mint extract and green food coloring and mix well.
2. To layer, your trifles use 2 mini trifle bowls or 2 glasses. Start with chopped oreo cookies and Aero mint chocolate in each trifle bowl. Top with pudding. I used 1 pudding snack in each trifle bowl. Top with York minis and more crumbled oreo cookies. Spoon the whipping cream and finish with an oreo cookie on top if preferred.

29

Velvet truffles

ingredients:-

- 1 box red velvet cake mix, and ingredients to make the cake
- 1 (16-ounce) can of prepared cream cheese frosting or homemade cream cheese frosting
- 1 pound white candy coating, or dark chocolate
- Sprinkles, to taste, or small candies to decorate, optional

Procedure:-

1. Prepare and bake the red velvet cake mix according to the directions of the package for a 9-inch by 13-inch cake.
2. Once baked, allow the cake to cool completely.
3. Crumble the cake into a large bowl and work it with your hands until it is in small pieces.
4. If desired, reserve a few spoonfuls of crumbs to use as decorative toppings on the finished truffles.
5. Spoon three-fourths of the frosting into the bowl and stir with a rubber spatula until the mixture is well combined.
6. It should be very moist and hold together if you squeeze a ball of cake between your fingers, but not too wet or greasy.
7. If the cake mixture is still a bit dry, add more frosting to reach the desired consistency.

8. Using a small cookie or candy scoop, scoop out small balls of cake and roll between your palms until they are round.
9. Place the cakes balls on a baking sheet covered with aluminum foil and refrigerate them while you prepare the candy coating.
10. Place the candy coating in a medium microwave-safe bowl and microwave it until melted, stirring after every 45 seconds to prevent overheating.
11. Using dipping tools or a fork, submerge a cake ball in the melted candy coating.
12. Remove it from the coating and drag the bottom across the lip of the bowl to remove excess coating.
13. Replace the dipped truffle on the foil-covered baking sheet.
14. If desired, top it with a sprinkle of cake crumbs, small candies, or other decorations while the coating is still wet. Repeat with remaining cake balls.
15. Refrigerate the truffles to set the coating completely, about 20 minutes.
16. These cake truffles are best served at room temperature and can be stored in an airtight container in the refrigerator for up to a week.

30

Bleberry pies

ingredients:-

- 1 recipe Pastry
- ¾ cup sugar
- 3 tablespoon cornstarch
- ⅛ teaspoon salt
- 1 cup water
- 4 cups fresh blueberries
- 1 tablespoon butter
- Fresh blueberries, sweetened whipped cream, and/or finely shredded lemon peel (optional)
- Sweetened whipped cream

Procedure:-

1. Preheat oven to 450 degrees F. Prepare Pastry. Divide chilled pastry into 8 portions. On a lightly floured surface roll each portion into a 7-inch circle. Line eight 4-3/8- to 5-inch foil or metal tart pans with pastry. Fold the edge under and crimp. Prick the bottom and sides of the pastry with a fork. Line with a double thickness of foil. Place on baking sheet. Bake for 8 minutes. Remove foil and bake for 4 to 6 minutes more or until browned. Cool on the wire rack.

2. Meanwhile, in a medium saucepan combine sugar, cornstarch, and salt. Stir in water and 1-1/2 cups of the blueberries. Cook and stir over medium heat until thickened. Remove from heat. Stir in the remaining 2-1/2 cups of blueberries and butter until the butter is melted. Cool completely. Pour into pie shell. If desired, cover and chill in the refrigerator until ready to serve.
3. To serve top with fresh berries, whipped cream, and lemon peel. Makes 8 mini pies.